# Table of Contents

PART 1: INTRODUCTION .....................................................

PART 2: GETTING TO KNOW ROVINJ ...............................

PART 3: CHURCH OF ROVINJ ..................................................................................6

PART 4: CULTURE IN *ROVINJ* ...............................................................................10

PART 5: FARMERS MARKET IN *ROVINJ* ..............................................................14

PART 6: SUMMER FESTIVAL IN *ROVINJ* .............................................................16

PART 7: TRAVELING TO *ROVINJ* ..........................................................................22

PART 8: IS *ROVINJ* EXPENSIVE? ...........................................................................25

PART 9: MAIN SQUARE IN *ROVINJ* ......................................................................27

PART 10: ISLANDS AROUND *ROVINJ* ..................................................................29

PART 11: ROVINJ SUNSET .......................................................................................32

PART 12: ROVINJ RESTAURANTS ..........................................................................36

PART 13: *ROVINJ* COCKTAIL BARS ......................................................................41

PART 14: BEACHES IN *ROVINJ* .............................................................................47

PART 15: POPULAR DESTINATIONS OUTSIDE OF *ROVINJ* ............................51

PART 16: EVENTS IN *ROVINJ* ................................................................................55

PART 17:  ACCOMMODATIONS IN *ROVINJ* ........................................................59

PART 18: OVERVIEW ................................................................................................66

# Part 1: Introduction

Have you ever been to a place that immediately puts a smile on your face? A place that warms your heart knowing that you have made it to that special place that makes you appreciate life. A place that automatically relieves you from all your stresses and worries that life is constantly throwing at us, from all different angles. It is like finally making it past an obstacle and reaching the finish line. A sense of feeling like "I made it." That is what Rovinj does to people, especially me. Growing up having spent my summers in Rovinj had always been the most memorable and happiest time in my childhood, as well as in my adulthood. It is a place that holds so many amazing memories and moments in my life, that I will forever cherish. Having gone there so often as a child allows me to appreciate it that much more. Not only the views, but the culture, the atmosphere, and most importantly the people. All of these aspects have a strong impact on how I have come to feel this way about a city. With that being said, those feelings will forever stay with me. The love and admiration for this city are what guided me in being able to write this book. When you are passionate about something, it gives you that much more motivation in being able to accomplish anything you put your mind to.

## Part 2: Getting to know ROVINJ

**Rovinj** (pronounced ro-VEEN) is a city on the western coast of the Istrian peninsula of Croatia. It is located on the north Adriatic Sea. This Venetian old town or in Croatian known as a "Stari Grad" is on a headland consisting of old houses and cobblestone streets leading to the church of St. Euphemia or Sveta Eufemija, at the top of the hill. Surrounding the old city of Rovinj is the breathtaking Cerulean Adriatic waters with many shades of blue. The harbor of Rovinj is surrounded by fishing boats, ferries, charter ships, and occasionally large yachts. In the summer months, these boats are constantly out on the water with tourists or with the locals, going out for a ride. Due to being so close to Italy, Rovinj to this day is a bilingual city, Croatian and Italian. Today, the locals continue to speak their distinct Croatian dialect with the Italian influence at home, keeping up with the old traditions. Rovinj was built during the Venetian Empire and later was taken over by the Austrians, Yugoslavians and today is part of the Republic of Croatia.

Due to the narrow streets and alleys in the old town, Rovinj is pedestrian-only. Many locals use bikes, scooters, or motorcycles to get around, while the rest simply go by foot on the cobblestone roads and stairs. The old town is picturesque filled with bright and vibrant colors along with the many houses all throughout. Each house is unique in its own beauty and history, allowing its charming look to flourish. The old town is filled with cafes, small boutiques, and many alleyways that take you to the water's edge. There is something just so romantic about this city, the beauty really grabs you. Rovinj itself has a wide variety of restaurants, cafes, bars, and ice cream shops, that are constantly flooded with people, during the warm months of the year especially.

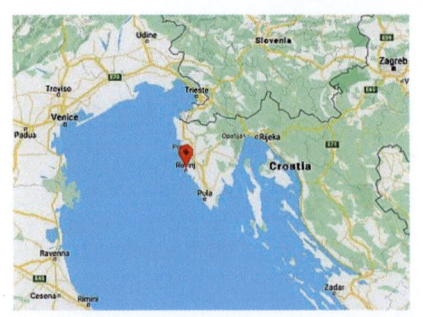

## Part 3: Church of Rovinj

The church of St. Euphemia was built in a Baroque style from 1725 until 1736 on top of an original church in its place. The iconic bell tower of the church was built earlier than the current standing church. It was built in the mid 1600's and resembles the tower in Venice, in St. Mark's Basilica. Rovinj is a major fishing port and a newly popular tourist destination. The city is slowly becoming well-known for its beauty from different movies or commercials that have been filmed there. The Hitman's Wife's Bodyguard, Diana and Heineken's the chase are just a couple that had been filmed in Rovinj. The old town of Rovinj was originally an island that was later connected to the mainland. Back when they were under Venetian rule in 1763 is when the island was connected, and the city began to further develop to what it is today.

As the story goes, Saint Euphemia was born in the year 290 in Chalcedon, a town in Asia Minor, today is known as Turkey. Euphemia was a young girl who was captured for continuing her practice of Christianity even with the threat of death. During this time under the rule of Tsar Diocletian, many Christians were captured, persecuted, and killed. At 15 years old, she was arrested by soldiers and tortured, for not giving up her religion of Christianity. The soldiers later then threw her to the lions and eventually she was killed. Her body was preserved by other Christian followers in Chalcedon but later her stone tomb or sarcophagus was thrown out to sea, once the city was taken over by the Persians.

Many years later, it is said that the tomb of Euphemia washed up on the shore of Rovinj. After many failed attempts, no one was able to bring her sarcophagus up to the then called church of Saint George. Finally, a young boy along with his two cows managed to haul the sarcophagus up the hill to the church on his own. The people of Rovinj were stunned and immediately believed this to be a miracle. The young boy is believed to have had a vision from Saint Euphemia, telling him that he would be able to bring up her tomb all on his own. After that miracle, the people of Rovinj proclaimed Saint Euphemia the patron saint of Rovinj.

The church of St. Euphemia is a white facade building with a beautiful bell tower to the left side of it. From the outside, the church looks simple and classic to a typical church built in that time. The inside of the church is a totally different story, much more elaborate than the outside. There are magnificent pillars all along the length of the church with spectacular statues and paintings all around. Above the main entrance of the church, there is a pipe organ which was built in 1754. The organ was built by a master organist Antonio Barbini, which has since kept most of its original structure. The alter itself is a sight to see. It is covered in marble and gold; consists of intricate statues of saints and angels. Behind the altar is a huge stone statue of their patron Saint Euphemia. The church also contains the relics of its patron saint; Saint Euphemia. To the side of the relics of Saint Euphemia, there are paintings on the wall which tell her story. The paintings portray the arrival of Saint Euphemia's relics to the city of Rovinj, as well as her martyrdom. The paintings explain how she came to be the patron saint for the city of Rovinj. On the ceiling of the church, there is a mural of the coronation of Saint Euphemia in the sky. All throughout the church, there are several other altars that are dedicated to other saints, that people may pray to on their visit to the church. The pews of the church are rustic looking with dark brown wood with soft red cushions. Visitors are still able to roam about the church during scheduled mass times. There are even designated pews in the back of the church for any visitors to come in, sit and pray during the mass. The feast day of their patron Saint Euphemia is on September 16th in commemoration of her martyrdom.

The bell tower has a statue of St. Euphemia at the top, which moves with the wind and acts as a weathervane. It is a total of 196 feet tall (60 meters), standing on the city's tallest hill. If you are already visiting and touring the church, climbing up the bell tower is a must. There is a total of 192 rickety steps leading up to the top of the bell tower in the church. The climb up is by far the most frightening thing due to the large gaps between each step and the creaking noises every step makes but is well worth the scare with the amazing views at the top. At the top of the bell tower, you can look out from all angles and get a great look at the city, the islands surrounding it, as well as other towns in the distance. The bell tower has a small fee to climb the tower but is justified with witnessing the impressive scenery. At the top, there are three bells that still ring at every hour throughout the day as a striking clock for the city. With that being said, it might not be the best idea to climb the bell tower at the top of the hour.

# Part 4: Culture in *Rovinj*

Rovinj, like every other European city, is laid back in their way of life and culture. It seems as though no one is ever in a rush; everyone always has the time to appreciate every moment. People enjoy their days and their lives to the fullest without hesitation. With that being said, everyone has time for a morning coffee with a friend or a loved one. Locals sit down at the nearby cafés and can sip on their espresso for hours. Those living in Rovinj, find the moment to simply cherish their time and not stress about what life might have thrown at them. During their morning coffees at the cafés, locals are not thinking about bills, finances, or any family problems they might have. They are there to get away from everything for a while, and just enjoy it. Drinking coffee at the café with a friend is a major part of every individual's culture and their day to day routine. It is a way for people to catch up, gossip, and have a good laugh with a friend. Every single café is full, all consisting of friends doing the same thing, socializing. Some people run off to work or any other obligation they might have, while others may remain there for hours. Since most of the houses in the old town of Rovinj are apartments, going out to the café with a friend is a great way to get out of the house rather than being cooped up inside. Typically, the older local men meet their friends at the café or even at the bar daily. Meeting at the same time and same place every day. They play different card games like Briscola (Briškula in Croatian) and Tresette (Trešeta in Croatian), all while drinking a coffee or glass of wine. They stay there till the same time each day; dinner time. Older women are typically housewives and cook at home all day waiting for their husbands and children to return. Traditionally, dinner in Rovinj and Croatia, in general, is very late especially during the summer months. Locals will eat dinner around eight or nine in the evening. This is an old farmer's custom that seems to have stuck with the people in Croatia and throughout Europe. Farmers would go back into the fields to do more work in their growing gardens once the sun started to go down, when it was no longer very hot. After they had finished their work for the day, they then had their late dinners back at home.

Since Rovinj is a city and is on the water, locals may have farmland that is further away from the city. Locals might live in the city but travel to their farmland daily to maintain and work on what they may be growing. Other individuals living in the city of Rovinj might not have any farmland at all, they might just simply work in the city and rely on fishing to have food for their families or to sell. Farmers in Rovinj are known for producing olive oil, wine, and truffles. The southwestern side of Istra is known for producing these particular items and is renowned all over Croatia especially, and in Europe. The climate and soil in that region of Istra are best for growing and producing olives and grapes. The Istrian peninsula is divided into three landscape zones. The west coast of Istra where Rovinj is located is known as "Red Istra" for having a red-brown soil called "Terra Rossa" soils that allows it to be very suitable for olive cultivation. A large majority of Istra's wine and olive oil distribution is grown in this region of Istra due to having that Terra Rossa soil.

The total population in Rovinj is over 14,000 people. That is a substantial amount of people for such a small city. The total area of the city is 75.5km$^2$ or 29.1mi$^2$. As in every other Croatian major city, there is a mix of ethnicities among the residents. The population of Rovinj includes over 75% of Croatians while the other 25% consists of ethnic minorities such as Italians, Serbians, Albanians, and Bosniaks. Many of those living in Rovinj that are not originally from there, came for a better opportunity for themselves as well as their families. Since Rovinj is highly populated with tourists in the summer, locals rely heavily on tourism to make a living. The climate in Rovinj is very mild due to the Mediterranean Sea, which allows this area to be a perfect spot for tourists to vacation. Summers are hot and dry, while the winters are mild and seemingly pleasant. The reason for this mild and essentially perfect weather is because the Mediterranean Sea is surrounded by land. Since it is not completely open water to the ocean, it allows the countries in that area to be mild. The coldest month of the year for Rovinj is in January, reaching a high of 50°F (10°C) and a low of about 41°F (5°C). The winters are the rainiest time of year for Rovinj especially, as well as other surrounding cities and countries on the Mediterranean. Rovinj and Croatia, in general, tends to not have much of an Autumn season, it typically goes from hot summer weather directly to a cooler temperature and into winter. With that being said, the Spring season comes earlier in Croatia than it would in other parts of the world.

# Part 5: Farmers Market in *Rovinj*

Like every European city, Rovinj has a farmers market in the city center in which locals are able to sell their locally grown produce, freshly caught seafood, and homemade items such as liquors and wine. The market is full of people every single day, especially early in the mornings. The mornings are the best time to go if you are looking for a specific item or food product. If you come to the market too late there is a chance that they will already be sold out of the item that you were interested in. Fishermen go out fishing early in the mornings and go straight to their stand at the market looking to sell their fresh fish. Locals are aware of the fact that they need to be at the market early in order to purchase a certain item or else they risk the chance of getting what they had wanted; that is why the mornings are the busiest time. The markets also have meat stands and a variety of cheese stands; all local individuals hoping to sell their home-grown products. Vendors also sell their homemade moonshine, known as "Rakija" or different handmade items such as souvenirs. Tourists love checking out and buying from these markets because they are guaranteed with the freshest and best products that were either caught from the sea or picked from the farm that very morning. They will always receive items that are well worth their money. Vendors selling at the market as always friendly and welcoming to all customers that come their way. They are always willing to help the customer find exactly what they are looking for and are able to explain the item in depth. These farmers markets continue to succeed and have many customers due to the fact that their items are cheaper than buying those same items from a standard supermarket. For tourists that are on a budget, it is worth shopping at the farmers market over any other store.

## Part 6: Summer Festival in Rovinj

Every summer, Rovinj hosts its summer festival or in Croatian called "Rovinjska Noć" meaning, the night of Rovinj. During this summer festival, people gather from all different towns and areas in the region of Istra. This particular festival is very widely known and always gathers a large crowd of people. All bars and restaurants are packed with locals and tourists, all enjoying the celebration with their friends and family. On the boardwalk or Riva, there is a huge stage prepared for the popular Croatian musician who will be performing there that evening for the festival. Rovinj always has a very well-known singer at their festival, which then draws a large crowd of people every year. Along the whole boardwalk, different vendors sell different items such as paintings they have made or many types of souvenirs. In front of the main stage, locals put on traditional Croatian performances in the city center. They perform their folklore or folklor dances in their traditional costumes. These performances usually consist of a boy and girl partner, while the sound of an accordion or bagpipe known as a "meh" is playing the music. Showing tourists these traditional dances allows them to get a feel for their culture and for the country's traditions as a whole.

Food and drinks are the main priority for a festival. A large variety of foods are served all night long. Different cafes and restaurants set up a stand to cook and serve people directly in the middle of the city's central square where the festival is held. There are different bars set up as well for different local winemakers to sell their wine by the glass or by the bottle. This is a great way for them to be able to self-advertise for their own home business. The main foods served at the different food stands are "ćevapi" which is minced meat, which looks like a small sausage; as well as hamburgers and "ražnjići" which is a meat skewer similar to the Greek Souvlaki. You can also find food stands that are serving fresh seafood such as grilled shrimp and octopus. Other stands serve a variety of pasta, some consisting of seafood, and others with locally grown truffle pasta or "Tartufi." Tartufi is local to the Istrian region and are very popular, but also very expensive to purchase. Also, during the summer festival, there are different food stands serving a variety of pastries and desserts.

Many people are selling fresh "Palačinke" made right in front of you or known as crepes. Other people make fresh "Fritule" known as fritters or zeppole. Locals and tourists walk around the city center, enjoying the live music and stop at the different stands for food and drinks. They roam around and find a place to sit and eat or can go watch the entertainment at the center stage, as they eat their food. Aside from food, locals also have shopping kiosks with souvenirs and handmade items available for purchase. Small children are entertained by the many toy stands, as well as the amusement rides and games that are also there during the festival. With that being said, there are many options for activities and things to see and do during a festival for people of all ages, both children and adults.

*Croatian style Palačinke / Crepes*

*Croatian style Ražnjići*

*Croatian style Ćevapi*

**Homemade fried Calamari**

Every year at midnight, the city hosts a spectacular firework show right in the center of the festival for all to see. These summer festivals last until the late hours in the night. The performance on the main stage lasts till around three in the morning or even later depending on who is singing. After midnight, different DJ booths are set up all around the city leading to an even longer party for the younger crowd especially. As the main performance comes to an end, the older crowd of people start to head home, leaving it now to a younger population. People continue to eat, drink, and dance for the rest of the night. The locals especially really enjoy this summer festival because it is always towards the end of August, leaving it as one of the last festivals of the summer.

## Part 7: Traveling to *Rovinj*

If you are going to travel to Rovinj, it is important to figure out the best way of transportation in getting there. The closest airport to Rovinj is the Pula International Airport. The airport is about 40 minutes away from Rovinj by car depending on which road you take. It is about 24-29 miles away (40-47km) from Rovinj's old town. It would be easiest to reserve a rental car at the airport and then drive to Rovinj from there. If you are not planning on leaving Rovinj during your trip, you might not want to have a car at all. There is a bus schedule from the airport to Rovinj. If you do fly into Pula, it would be a good idea to check the schedule beforehand so that you can plan accordingly in case the schedule does not work with your flight arrival time. The bus would be the cheapest option in transportation to Rovinj but might not work for everyone depending on their own flight schedules. There are many taxi drivers at Pula airport and will drive anywhere. This is not the cheapest option, it can be a bit pricey, but it is the most convenient option if the rental car and bus options do not work out. Picking out a way of transportation all depends on the way you plan to spend your overall time in Rovinj. If you plan to travel to other cities near Rovinj it would be most convenient to have a car with you. Another thing you must think about before making this overall decision is figuring out if you will have a place to park your car once you arrive to Rovinj. Since the entire old town is pedestrian-only, it might not be realistic for a tourist to have a rental car if they are staying in a hotel that is in the old town itself. Other hotels that are outside of the old town of Rovinj, have available parking for their guests. Deciding whether to rent a car during your trip would all depend on which hotel you choose to stay at.

If you are traveling from Italy, specifically Venice, it would definitely be easiest to take a ferry to Rovinj. There are two main ferry companies that run directly from Rovinj to Venice, Italy and vice versa. The two main ferry companies that connect these two cities are the Venezia Lines and the Adriatic Lines. Both lines are high-speed passenger catamarans that provide passengers with a comfortable experience. Both of the ferry company's journey from Rovinj to Venice takes around 3 hours or so. Each of the two companies takes a different route which makes the journey time difference between the two companies. Both lines sail every day of the week during the busy season and vary between three to four times a week during the slow seasons. Also, both ferry lines charge about the same amount per ticket. They range in price from 65 to 70 USD (61-65 Euro) for an adult ticket going one way. Taking the ferry to visit Rovinj or even to leave from Rovinj would be the best option in that you are taken directly to the city. The ferry would arrive or leave from Rovinj's harbor, which is directly in the city center, making it much easier as a traveler.

## Part 8: Is *Rovinj* Expensive?

Compared to other parts of the region of Istra, Rovinj is more expensive overall. Since it is one of the top tourist destinations in Istra and Croatia, Rovinj has the prices to reflect that. Croatia as a whole is not the most expensive country to visit in Europe which is part of the reason for a large increase in tourism over the last few years. Croatia is known for being affordable in pretty much every aspect such as food, drinks, travel, and accommodations. With that being said, certain cities are top tourist destinations and are the most expensive cities to visit. Rovinj is among those expensive cities, others being Dubrovnik and Hvar. These three cities, in particular, tend to have higher prices for just about everything, compared to areas in Croatia that are not as popular with tourists. If traveling to Rovinj on a budget, there are certainly ways that a traveler can save on their trip. The best way to save on your trip to Rovinj would be on your accommodations. If money is an issue, there are many options in finding cheaper accommodations such as booking through Airbnb or finding a private house or apartment to rent. Also, another way to save on a trip to Rovinj would be choosing a restaurant for dinner wisely. If on a budget, it is important to be mindful about which restaurant you choose to dine at. Of course, going to a bigger and more popular restaurant will be more expensive as opposed to other smaller restaurants. There are plenty of small and authentic taverns in Rovinj that you can find that are far less expensive and have equal or better food.

The Croatian Kuna or Hrvatska Kuna has been in use since 1994. Before using the Croatian Kuna, they had used the Croatian Dinar which was Croatia's first currency following the country's independence from the former country, Yugoslavia. When shopping in Croatia, some stores will show the prices both in Kuna as well as in Euros. Stores provide the prices in both currencies to make it easier for other European travelers. Also, some individuals in Croatia are even paid in Euro depending on what company they work for. As of 2013, Croatia has been the 28th member to join the European Union. Croatia has not yet changed its currency to the Euro but may obtain the new currency in the next few years. With that being said, some stores or individuals do accept Euro as a source of payment even though the currency is not officially Euros. The European Union was organized to unite all members in working as a single market in developing the economy especially. Although the European Union is meant to be beneficial and a positive thing for its members, not all Croatians find this to be true due to their new high taxes upon entering as a member into the Union. Citizens are struggling with the new taxes and fees that are now required of them.

    When exchanging your money, the best places to go are to any bank or even a money exchange service which is known as a **"Mjenjačnica" in Croatian**. There are many different banks and exchange places all over the city of Rovinj so it would not be an issue to exchange money. As of May 2020, 1, United States Dollar (USD) will get you 6.98 Kuna which is a great exchange rate at the moment. Typically, during the summer months, the exchange is a bit lower.

## Part 9: Main Square in *Rovinj*

The main square of Rovinj is known as Trg Maršala Tita or Marshal Tito square. This triangular city square is the center of Rovinj located right on the city's harbor. On one side of the square is the harbor while the other is the start of the old city, consisting of cafés, restaurants, and stores all around. This square is a great stopping point for locals passing through or tourists roaming the city. There is much to do in this square and a great spot to stop and relax to appreciate the beautiful view of the harbor. Tourists especially walk around with their gelato and stop there for a rest to just admire the scenery and the city itself. Any main event or festival to happen for the city of Rovinj takes place at this particular square. There are often concerts held at this square throughout the year for locals and tourists to enjoy and listen. On one side of the main square, there is a well-known and distinguished pink clock tower which is decorated with a Venetian lion. The clock tower was built in the Baroque-style like most of the rest of the city which is built in Venetian architecture. Directly in front of the clock tower and the middle of the city's main square is a fountain with a statue on top of a young boy holding a water-sprouting fish. The fountain was a way to commemorate the government-funded water system that had finally brought running water into the city of Rovinj in 1959. The fountain having a fish theme is very fitting for the overall culture of the city since it is a popular fishing port. To the other side of the fountain is the entrance gate into the old town itself, which is known as Balbi's Arch or Balbijev luk. Past the arch is the start of Grisia Street which leads up to the church of Saint Euphemia.

# Part 10: Islands around *Rovinj*

While staying in Rovinj, you might want to consider visiting one of the many islands surrounding the city. There are a total of 22 beautiful islands and islets surrounding the entire city of Rovinj that are easily accessible by water taxi. The closest island to Rovinj is the island of Saint Katarina or in Croatian, Otok Sveta Katarina. Boats leave regularly from Rovinj's harbor to the island of Katarina since it is so close. The ride takes about 10 minutes and is perfect for a day trip if you want to get out of the city and just enjoy the beach for the day. There is only one hotel on the entire island called Island Hotel Katarina, which is built alongside an old castle and that has been integrated into the hotel. The island has breathtaking views of the old town of Rovinj, the park of Zlatni Rat, and the archipelago surrounding Rovinj. The hotel offers a large variety of water sports and provides guests with many different sporting games to enjoy such as tennis and beach volleyball. The island has many spots with high rocks that are great for adventurous people to jump off into the blue sea. Even if you do not plan on jumping off the rocks, it is still worth the visit up to enjoy the spectacular view from the top.

The second most popular island that surrounds Rovinj is Crveni Otok or Red Island. The island consists of two islets connected by an embankment. The two islets are called Sveti Andrija (St. Andrew) and Maškin. It is about a 20-minute boat ride from the harbor in Rovinj. The total coast for a round trip by boat is 40 Kuna or about 6 USD. Cars are not allowed on either part of Red Island, so it is a more relaxing vibe, with just the sound of the wind and the waves crashing onto the pebbled beach. There is a lot of water activities to be enjoyed on either islet such as sailing, windsurfing, diving, snorkelling and of course swimming. The island consists mainly of stone beaches and coves covered with pebbles. Many of those beaches have high rocks which are great for diving and jumping into the sea. Since the island is small, tourists can walk the entire island in about 40 minutes to explore and find a nice cove to lay down and tan, as well as to swim. The smaller island Maškin does not have any hotels itself, but since it is so close to Sveti Andrija tourists can walk the island even if they are staying at the hotel on the Sveti Andrija side of the island. The islet of Maškin is mostly covered in pines making it beautiful for walks along the beach. The islet of Sveti Andrija has one main hotel called Island Hotel Istra. The hotel is the only business running on the entire island, leaving it the only option for tourists to visit if they require a restaurant, shop or place to spend the night.

# Part 11: ROVINJ sunset

Everyone has seen a beautiful sunset in their life before. But you have not experienced a magical and romantic sunset until you have seen a sunset in Rovinj. This seafront city is the perfect location for one to feel as if they are living in the sunset itself. At the time of sunset, locals and tourists race and line up on the boardwalk or "Riva" to catch the magnificent sight. The sunset is known for lingering over the horizon until it finally falls into the water and leads to darkness. People gather with their loved ones to enjoy the beautiful sight while sitting up on the stone wall along the water. Many take photos and videos to capture the moment. The sunset itself is a striking mixture of colors that almost looks like a painting. In a way, it almost looks fake, from how perfect the colors in the sky are formed. What makes the sunset even more eye-catching is the view of the old town. The old town of Rovinj is highlighted as if there were a spotlight shining on it, making it stand out even more than it already did. Every stone house and rooftop are instantaneously more noticeable, and its beauty is even more apparent. The variety of colored houses are instantly brightened while almost looking neon from the bright streaming sunlight. Behind the old town is, of course, the changing colors from the sunset in the sky. At first a bright yellow and orange take over the sky which then leads to a darker blue and red color. As the sky starts turning to that dark blue and red color, the old town itself starts to disappear into darkness until finally, the city goes dark, only leaving the outline of the houses and church tower. While everyone is gathered on the Riva, it feels as if everyone is frozen at that moment. The sunset is mesmerizing enough to let you forget about life for a short time and lets you focus on the beauty before your eyes. While sitting and watching the sunset, there is a silence among the observers. At that moment, no one has anything to say. They are all in awe by the sight before them that there are no words to even describe how they are feeling. In that brief period of beauty, it is as if there is nothing else going on in the world or in that time. It is as if nothing else matters but what is in front of you. Rovinj's sunsets are a popular moment for men to take the view as a chance to propose to their loved ones. With a view that majestic, how could they say no to their partner's proposal? At the moment of dusk, the crowd goes back to chatter and movement, and back to reality. From being frozen, to instantly back to their physical existence and alert with their surroundings. The crowd goes on with their evening and away from the seafront all in a matter of seconds as if nothing had ever happened. A sunset must be worth witnessing if the entire city stops and stands still for those few minutes of bliss.

# Part 12: ROVINJ Restaurants

**Monte**

The restaurant Monte was first opened in Rovinj in 2008. The restaurant is run by a husband and wife team, known as Danijel and Tjitske Djekic. Danijel is the owner and head chef, while Tjitske is the restaurant's hostess. It is located in the old town on Ulica Montalbano which is a minute walk from the church of Saint Euphemia. It is Croatia's first-ever Michelin Star restaurant and was awarded to Monte in 2017. Since Monte's well deserved and prestigious award, there have been six other restaurants in Croatia to receive the same award. The Dutch and Croatian restaurateurs, Danijel and Tjitske go out daily to the local farmers markets to find the freshest and best produce, seafood, and meats for their menu. They pride themselves in being able to obtain the best items and ingredients for their upscale menu. This award has made an advance in Croatian cuisine as a whole, allowing the country to be recognized for their food in more of a non-traditional approach. Monte has exquisite food, which is paired with great local and foreign wines, especially those from the local area of Rovinj and the region of Istra. The waiters are knowledgeable in every aspect of the menu and cuisine itself and are all presented professionally. The food presentation is creative and contemporary. On the menu, customers are given the options from the "Degustacija" menu which is a tasting menu where customers can choose the six courses they would like to have, based on a set price. The menu is also divided by color into three separate menu options in different sections based on different types of food pairings such as seafood or meat. Customers are also given the option to create their menu of selecting three courses from any of the three separate menus for a cheaper set price. There are also over 100 wine options found on the wine menu to accompany their meals. Although this restaurant is on the pricey side, customers will indefinitely leave feeling thrilled by their overall experience and meals from the freshness and unforgettable taste.

## La Perla

The restaurant La Perla is rated 4.5-stars serving a Mediterranean cuisine. This authentic and traditional restaurant serves amazing seafood dishes that are fresh from the Adriatic Sea. The local owners, the Ruzic family, and staff members make your dining experience all the more special with their welcoming attitudes and enthusiasm in serving their customers. It is located on the street called Ulica Egidia Bullessicha which is about a thirteen-minute walk from the Riva or boardwalk of Rovinj, or about a three-minute drive. Since this restaurant is not in the city center, more locals are found to dine here than tourists. With that being said, it is still easy for tourists to reach La Perla from the old town of Rovinj. The restaurant itself is very close to the sea which makes it perfect for an after-dinner stroll to catch the romantic sunset with your loved ones. Beautiful indoor and outdoor seating giving you a rustic vibe making it all the more traditional. A mix of rustic and modern twists of furniture throughout the restaurant. The menu is fairly priced, and customers receive large portions of their meals. The restaurant provides customers with a large parking lot outside as well as a play area for children.

**Calisona Restaurant**

     The restaurant Calisona is a family-owned restaurant working over three generations and 70 years of service. Its newly renovated interior has a mix of Istrian tradition mixed with a modern feel. The restaurant Calisona is located just outside the city gate, Balbi's arch, which is right near the city's central square. It is positioned at another square called Trg na Mostu. This particular square is known for once being the site of the medieval draw bridge which connected the original island of Rovinj to the mainland. The restaurant is perfectly positioned within the city's center on the corner of the famous street called Carera Ulica. Many locals and tourists shop on this particular street which leads directly to the restaurant, allowing it to be easily accessible for everyone to get to. The restaurant has a large outdoor seating area, making it inviting to tourists who stroll through the square. The menu is a mix of Italian and Mediterranean cuisine, mostly focusing on seafood.

# Part 13: *Rovinj* Cocktail bars

**Valentino Cocktail and Champagne Bar**

Valentino Cocktail and Champagne Bar is one of Rovinj's most popular bars in the old town which has been open since 1989. The bar is attractive to both locals and tourists because of its beautiful placement literally on the rocks overlooking the water. Valentino Bar is positioned on the southwest side of the old town of Rovinj, overlooking the water. It is a short five-minute walk from the church of Saint Euphemia. Customers are provided with a light blue cushion and given a spot on the rocks to enjoy the magnificent view along with a cocktail of their choice. Valentino bar is more and more popular each year, leaving it full at all times of the day and night. It is especially busy during sunset particularly in the warmer months of the year. Customers sit on their cushions and enjoy the sunset while boats sail back to the city's harbor. It is a romantic spot to get close to the one you love while sipping on a cocktail as the water crashes up onto the rocks. Throughout the flat parts of the rocks, large candlesticks are lighting up the area that sets the mood and makes it that much more romantic. The bar places underwater lights that allow the water to have a vivid cerulean color all night long even after the sun has set. This adds to the overall atmosphere and gives customers that romantic energy. There are many different cocktails and drinks available on Valentino's menu. They are known specifically for their Aperol Spritz and Moët & Chandon champagne. Drinks are overpriced but customers do not seem to mind considering the magnificent view and overall ambiance of the bar.

**Mediterraneo Bar**

  Mediterraneo Bar is another popular bar that is situated on the waterfront of Rovinj. It is right next door to the Valentino bar, giving it a similar yet different vibe. Mediterraneo bar has a more laid back and relaxed atmosphere. There are brightly colored tables and chairs throughout the patio on the rocks. The staff are all friendly and inviting, willing to make your experience that much more remarkable. The staff is willing to help all customers in being able to find the perfect drink based on their preferences. It is extremely cozy with cushions and funky chair sizes and shapes making it more of a rustic look and feel. There are cute and fun quotes scattered throughout the bar either on the tables and chairs themselves or signs hanging on the stone walls. The quotes are either nautical themed or they make a coffee and cocktail reference. On each of the tables, there is a beautiful flower arrangement creating an even more rustic and cute atmosphere. Customers can choose from the elaborate cocktail or coffee list. There are many options for allowing everyone to find the right cocktail choice for themselves. Customers can take a swim into the sea if they wish to, and then return to their table to finish their coffees or cocktails. This bar is again a bit on the pricey side but is worth the price for the view and overall comfort. Mediterraneo Bar is also about a five-minute walk up to the church of Saint Euphemia. This bar is a must-see if you are looking for a more relaxed coffee or cocktail experience with a spectacular view of the sea.

**Wine Bar Tomasso**

Another great place that has a wonderful view of the city of Rovinj as well as one of the best places to go for a cocktail is San Tomasso Vinoteka Enoteca; or also known as Wine Bar Tomasso. This wine bar is a perfect spot to relax while enjoying the lovely view of the harbor and the city of Rovinj. The wine bar is positioned directly across the harbor from Marshal Tito Square, giving customers a great view of the main square and the fountain. This is an ideal spot for a wine bar, customers are amazed by the view. The wine bar is open early in the morning for coffee and stays open late for food and cocktails. Inside the wine bar, it gives you a rustic feel with wood panels and stone everywhere. The menu offers customers a selection of appetizers, desserts, ice creams, and of course the wine list. They are known for their house wine, which is from the San Tomasso winery in Bale, Istra. They also offer other known wines from the region of Istra, as well as other parts of Croatia and Italy.

# Part 14: Beaches in *Rovinj*

**Mulini Beach**

Mulini Beach is a popular beach that is located directly in front of Rovinj's luxurious hotel, Monte Mulini. Taking the path along the harbor, the beach is just a short 15-minute walk from the old town of Rovinj. The beachfront itself was completed in 2014, consisting of a mixture of pebbled areas and modern concrete plateaus leading down to the water. The beach itself consists of a pebble beach which directly leads to the water, for a large portion of the beachfront. The other portion of the beach consists of natural stone slabs which makes it much easier for sunbathing as well as much easier to get in and out from the water. This beach has water entrances with stairs that lead into the water, along with hand railings to make it much easier for swimmers to get into and out of the water. Beachgoers will find this beach to be very convenient and easily accessible to everyone. The concrete floor areas are more comfortable for laying down and tanning as opposed to laying down on the uncomfortable rocks or pebbles. This beach is not private to the hotel, all visitors are welcome to the beach and even to the beach bar located right on the beachfront in between the beach and the hotel. Closer to the beach bar and the hotel, tourists can rent umbrellas, chairs, or cabanas to enjoy their beach day in comfort. For those who are staying at the hotel, the prices for beach supplies are included in their hotel fees allowing them to use any service that they wish to choose. The beach bar area provides visitors with all the amenities that they may need, such as toilets, changing rooms, and showers. The bar itself offers a great variety of foods, impressive cocktails, and soft drinks. In the evenings, the bar transforms into a more intimate lounge area with a cozy atmosphere along the water.

**Lone bay beach**

    Another wonderful beach located just outside the city center of Rovinj is Lone Bay Beach. This is the most visited of all beaches in Rovinj by tourists and residents to the area, it is located just past Mulini beach. The graveled beach makes it easier for swimmers to walk in and out of the water and especially easier and safer for families with children. The beach has available chairs and umbrellas for rent throughout the day. The beach is situated right near the entrance for Zlatni Rat or Golden Cape Park, which also gives beachgoers the option to layout under the trees for some shade. Along the beach, people have many rental options in different activities to do besides swimming which include surfboards, paddle boats, canoes, along with other beach amenities. The beach also has a beach bar and restaurants for visitors to enjoy a refreshment or food on the beach. The beach is easily accessible from the old town of Rovinj, just over a 20-minute walk both on the beach harbor path or a route which is more inland. For those staying in the old town of Rovinj, it would be more convenient to walk rather than drive a car to this beach. The nearest parking lot to Lone Bay Beach is about a 10-minute walk to the beach, leaving it not much longer to simply walk to the beach itself. The beach gives you an incredible glimpse of the old town of Rovinj in the distance, as well as the island of Katarina which is directly in front of the beach. Lone bay beach is worth the visit for its convenience for all age groups and its natural beauty and spectacular views.

**Cuvi Beach**

Cuvi beach is another popular and impressive beach just outside of Rovinj that is filled with tourists and locals throughout the summer months. Cuvi beach is even further south from the other two beaches mentioned. It is just under 2 miles (3 kilometers) south which would take tourists about a 12-minute drive and around a 25-minute walk from the old town of Rovinj to get to Cuvi beach. The beach consists of areas with rocks and gravel and also different areas containing small pebbles. Having beaches like this makes things suitable for families with small children so that they can play, as well as making it easier to get to and from the water. The beach has very clear blue and green water which is not deep unless you are to go all the way out. Having shallow and calm water is perfect for children and even adults to play different water games and activities. Like Lone bay beach, Cuvi beach has many shaded areas under the trees for individuals to get away from the sun. Cuvi beach bar is a great spot for those at the beach to stop and unwind for a bit while enjoying a coffee or some food. The beach is further away from all the action of the city which allows it to have a more relaxing and peaceful atmosphere.

# Part 15: Popular destinations outside of *Rovinj*

**Zlatni Rat Forest Park (Golden Cape)**

If you want to explore the area and get out of the city and enjoy some nature, the best place to visit is Zlatni Rat Forest Park (Golden Cape). Just a short 15-minute walk south from the city of Rovinj, you are in a whole new world. It was declared a National Park in 1961 and has been a popular natural attraction in Rovinj ever since. Zlatni Rat is the oldest protected area in the region of Istra because of the high botanical area found within the park as a whole. The Golden Cape is an ideal place for a variety of different sporting activities, such as running, walking, and cycling. Those exercising in the park do not have to worry about oncoming traffic or cars since the entire area is closed off from all vehicles. Since the park is situated on a cape, the beach is not far from the park trail itself. The beaches are mainly pebbly and rocky coves in every part of the cape. The pebbles lead to a shallow crystal-clear blue water that quickly turns deep. Pebble stone beaches are perfect for people to lay down and enjoy the view of the sea. Also found on the cape are rocks that are perfect for climbing.

**Limski Kanal**

About 5 miles (7.5 Km) north of Rovinj, there is a bay called Limski Kanal or Lim Bay. Lim Bay is one of the most magnificent natural resources in the Istrian Peninsula. The bay is about 6.2miles long, 0.37miles wide and 98 feet deep (10 Km long, 600m wide and 30m deep). If staying in Rovinj, visiting Limski Kanal would be a nice little trip away from the city. The bay is only a 15-minute drive from the city of Rovinj which would give tourists a nice scenic spot far enough from the busy city. Also, there are boat tours that take you directly to Limski Kanal from Rovinj's port. Those visiting the bay can either hike or bike ride through the forest. There is a restaurant at the mouth of the canyon called Restaurant Viking. This waterside restaurant serves fresh seafood especially oysters and mussels which are farmed in the bay itself and caught daily. This is a wonderful place to eat and enjoy the view of the bay especially after a long hike or bike ride through the forest along the bay. This is a great place to spend a few hours of your day before heading back to your hotel or apartment in Rovinj.

**Heritage Museum**

When visiting a new city, it is also important to learn about the culture and history that goes along with it. Rovinj's Heritage Museum is a perfect place for tourists to learn about history as well as view a variety of artwork. The museum was founded in 1954 by a group of artists all from Rovinj. The museum has a large assortment of items that have been collected over the years, including modern art, archaeological findings, ethnology, documents, books, and photographs. All items found in the museum can tell a story about a different part of the history involving Rovinj including both current events and more ancient events and history. The museum is in a prime spot located right in the city center of Rovinj on the main square of Marshall Tito. Visiting this museum is a great option to do during the day on a trip to Rovinj since it is in the center and extremely convenient to get to. The museum entrance fee is only 15 Kuna which is about $2 for adults and 10 Kuna for children. This is especially great for tourists if it happens to be a rainy day on their trip to Rovinj, might as well learn and view the history of the beautiful city.

# Part 16: Events in *Rovinj*

## GRISIA

The street or "Ulica" called Grisia is picturesque with cobblestone pathways leading up directly to the church of Saint Euphemia. The street of Grisia is filled with galleries and different souvenir shops all displaying their work both inside their stores and outside along the walls of the buildings. Artists are always showcasing their drawings, paintings, and sculptures for tourists to view and purchase. Most of the artist's focal point for their artwork is the magnificent views and sights of Rovinj itself. Since this particular street is already highly populated with artists, is the reason for Rovinj's open-air art exhibition to be named after the street itself "Grisia." This one-day art competition exhibition first started in August 1967 by the Rovinj Heritage Museum and has been held every August ever since. The exhibition is always held on the second Sunday of August every summer. This is a great opportunity for professional and even amateur artists to get recognition and have their artwork seen by potential buyers. Artists who have their studios on the street of Grisia open their doors for the public and welcome any viewers or customers to have a browse throughout their studios. Other artists showcase their work of art on the ancient city walls, doors, stairs, and windows of Rovinj's old town. The exhibitions start down at the bottom of the hill by Balbi's Arch or "Balbijev Luk" and work its way up the winding streets to the church. The streets are packed with tourists and locals all slowly making their way up the hill while admiring and observing all the variety of artwork.

**Rovinj Summer Festival**

Rovinj has several music festivals that run through the summer, along with its annual town festival that is held in late August. In July, Rovinj hosts a weekend-long Salsa Festival that takes place in over 10 different locations scattered around Rovinj. There are a few different hotels, clubs, and outdoor city spots that take part in this festival every year. There are also boat parties that sail around Rovinj, as well as boat parties that take you to the island of Sveta Katarina where the event continues. Each different location organizes its own event during the salsa festival. They organize different musicians or DJs for their location and arrange salsa dance workshops for people to learn and join in alongside the professional instructors. The hotels that are involved in this event typically create a salsa pool party during the day consisting of the same idea of providing salsa dance workshops. This event is a great way for people to have fun, let loose and dance. The Salsa Festival also takes place in the Croatian city of Opatija, typically a week before Rovinj's event. All tickets are sold online, as well as in designated areas on the day of the event.

Rovinj also hosts an event called "Summer music festival" which also takes place at different locations and different days throughout the city. Some locations include Porton

Biondi Beach and Crveni Otok. The festival's schedule includes different Croatian artists as well as artists from other countries, involved in genres like pop, jazz, and soul. All scheduled events during this festival provides food and drink options available for purchase for the crowd of people to choose from. This event is known for bringing a large attendance of people either to see an artist they already love or those who are looking to listen to new music. All tickets are sold online before the day of each scheduled show.

## Half Marathon

Every year the city of Rovinj hosts a half marathon called Rovinjski polumaraton or Rovinj Half Marathon. The half marathon in Rovinj usually takes place in spring, sometime in April. The half marathon starts and finishes on the main square of Rovinj, Trg Maršala Tita. The marathon route varies, first starting in a more scenic area overlooking the water, then the trail heads through the old city, and even leads through forest area and even passes a more residential area. Runners have an entry fee of 120 Kuna or about $17. The run is usually in the morning, and the award ceremony is held around One in the afternoon once all of the runners have finished. Included in the entry fee is a T-shirt, a chip timer, refreshments throughout the course and after, and lunch once the race is complete. Prize money, medals, and trophies are given to the first five men and women to finish the race. This event truly must be an incredible view, while running a marathon and having Rovinj's spectacular city right in front of you must be amazing to experience.

# Part 17: Accommodations in *Rovinj*
**Hotel Adriatic**

When staying in Rovinj, one of the most important aspects of your trip is the accommodation you choose. The luxurious boutique hotel, Hotel Adriatic is the most special place you could stay in Rovinj. The hotel combines a modern character while keeping up with its historical and vintage vibe. The hotel has spectacular views from all sides. One side overlooks the harbor, to the left is the main square of Rovinj, "Marshall Tito Square" and the right side is the old town view of the church of Saint Euphemia. The positioning of the hotel could not be more central to everything that Rovinj has to offer. The church of Saint Euphemia is about a 9-minute walk from the hotel. One of the nearest beaches, Monte Mulini is also not so far from the hotel, guests would have to walk about 15-minutes or so. As for everything else that Rovinj offers to their tourists, is only a short walk away from the hotel. This hotel is Rovinj's oldest hotel and its building dates from 1892. Massive renovations took place in 2015, giving it a more modern feel but continues to maintain its original facade and vintage charm.

There is a total of 14 rooms and 4 suites which all vary in size and arrangement. The hotel provides free Wi-Fi, free parking, and continental breakfast to all guests. The hotel has a French brasserie inspired restaurant located on the ground level which offers guests delicious and fresh Mediterranean cuisine. At "Brasserie Adriatic" guests also have the option to sit out on the terrace which overlooks the harbor or inside in the dining room among the green velvet armchairs dining decor. The hotel's "Cafe Adriatic" is perfect for after-dinner drinks and dessert or those looking for a classic cocktail or whiskey. There is outdoor seating all along the length of the hotel for guests to enjoy the view and the hustle of the city streets all while enjoying a cake and drink.

**Grand Park Hotel Rovinj**

Another great hotel option for a trip to Rovinj would be Grand Park Hotel. This hotel is definitely on the pricey side but would be worth the splurge especially if staying in Rovinj for a special occasion, such as a honeymoon. Grand Park Hotel is elegant with contemporary architecture that is settled within a centuries-old pine forest. It is a six-floor hotel that slopes down towards the sea, each floor consisting of wood and glass walls giving it a more modern feel. There are a total of 209 rooms and suites that are each spectacular and elegant in its own way.

The hotel is just outside of the city center, about a mile away (1.8km), and would take around 15-minutes to walk to from the center. This luxury, 5-star hotel gives guests a magnificent view of the old town, the island of Sveta Katarina, and of course the Adriatic Sea. The hotel provides guests with many different amenities to make their stay that much more enjoyable. Guests have the option to swim in either their indoor or outdoor pool, use of the fitness center, spa, and beach access. There is a convenient airport shuttle that guests can reserve beforehand that drives them directly to the hotel from any of the airports located in Croatia. There is also free parking as well as free Wi-Fi on the premises. The hotel has four different restaurants and two bars and a patisserie that guests can choose from. Each of the restaurants and bars has a glass wall terrace for guests to be able to have a spectacular view of Rovinj while enjoying their meals and cocktails. Guests staying at this hotel have everything they could need for their stay in Rovinj. Guests would without a doubt love every moment of their stay at Grand Park Hotel.

**Hotel Spirito Santo Palazzo Storico**

This last hotel option is a boutique-style located in the actual old town of the city of Rovinj. Hotel Spirito Santo Palazzo Storico is nestled within Rovinj's dreamy old town historical buildings. The hotel is about a 6-minute walk from the church of Saint Euphemia. The location is ideal in being able to experience the old town feel and a more tranquil atmosphere that is away from busier pathways around the church and the main squares. The hotel gains popularity for its rustic charm architecture that is combined with its modern furnishing. If you are interested in a hotel that is not as busy and provides a small, cozy, and romantic atmosphere, then Hotel Spirito Santo Palazzo Storico is the perfect fit for you. There is a total of seven guest rooms in this boutique hotel, each of the rooms differ in size but all have similar details of hardwood flooring and exposed rafters. The hotel has a lounge bar that has beautiful exposed bricks, where guests can sit and sip on a glass of local wine or a cocktail of their choice. Guests also have the option of sitting outside on the romantic candle-lit terrace with the view of the church of Saint Euphemia. Out of the three hotel suggestions, this hotel is the cheapest but certainly does not lack in any way compared to the others.

There are hundreds of different hotels in Rovinj that tourists can book for their trip. For travelers that are not willing to spend a great deal on their accommodations, there are plenty of different cheaper options available. Private home or apartment rentals are very popular in Rovinj and throughout Europe. If you are looking for a great deal in accommodations, then renting a private apartment or house is the best option. There are numerous advertisements and websites online that show the listings of different apartments and housing available in Rovinj. Using sites like Airbnb, allow the traveler to get a great view of the rental options and can filter their searches based on their price range and what exactly they are looking for. Renting out an apartment or house is far less expensive than renting a room at a large commercial hotel. By renting an apartment within the old town of Rovinj, tourists can truly get a feel of the way of life for the locals who live there. Also, if you are traveling on a budget these apartments and houses, of course, all come with a kitchen so a traveler could be saving even more money by simply preparing some of their meals rather than eating out. Also, Rovinj has high rated hostels that are great especially for backpackers and for those who are not looking to spend a great amount on their accommodation while on their trip.

## Part 18: Overview

Hopefully, this little guide will inspire you and assist you in being able to plan your trip to the unbelievably stunning Croatian city of Rovinj. Rovinj is such a picturesque and magical city that should be visited by all tourists that are planning trips in Europe, and more specifically in Croatia. This guide will hopefully give travelers some insight into what the best-rated places are to see or stay around Rovinj, which is all taken into consideration through personal experience. All items listed in this guide were visited and have been experienced, leaving this book's suggestions to be considered mostly through personal preference and observation of these different locations and sights hands-on. With that being said, hopefully, this guide will allow you to also have an amazing trip and overall experience in the city that brings joy and excitement to me personally.

Printed in Great Britain
by Amazon